MW00989347

Chu Gar Gao

Southern Praying Mantis

Hakka Kungfu

像遺公師水劉

觀音閣
**Grandteacher,
Lao Siu, trained
Chu Gar Mantis,
circa 1910,
at this Guan Yin,
Goddess of Mercy
Temple,
on the
East River,
Huiyang, China.**

東江

East River

5 Volumes
10 Years Ongoing Research

China Southern
Praying Mantis Kungfu Survey™

Volume 1
Pingshan Mantis Celebration

Volume 2
China Mantis Reunion

Volume 3
Kwongsai / Iron Ox Interviews

Volume 4
On Monk Som Dot's Trail

Volume 5
Chu Gar Mantis Celebrations

Also available!
5 volumes in one multimedia eBook!

派螂螳家朱

Chu Gar Gao

Southern Praying Mantis Hakka Kungfu

Featuring
Late Sifu Cheng Wan

By
Roger D. Hagood

Charles Alan Clemens, Editor

Southern Mantis Press | Pingshan Town, China

Southern Mantis Press
462 W. Virginia St. (Rt. 14)
Crystal Lake, Illinois 60014
1-800-Jook Lum
books@southernmantispress.com

Ordering Information:
Special discounts are available for martial art schools, bookstores, specialty shops, museums and events.   Contact the publisher at the address above.

Cover photographs: The late Grandteacher of Chu Gar Mantis in Hong Kong, Cheng Wan, and his son, Sifu Cheng Chiu.

Cheng Chiu photography by Micah Chiang Photography, Hong Kong, www.micahchiang.com

ISBN: 978-0-9857240-2-3

Dedication

The author and late Grandmaster Cheng Wan, right

Late Sifu Cheng Wan

Every year for 35 years, in the summer, Cheng Sifu held Chu Gar Mantis celebrations with hundreds of International kungfu teachers, students, laymen, and laywomen in attendance. They were grand traditional kungfu celebrations of the old type.

Each summer celebration began with unicorn and lion dancing, swearing in of new members, kungfu demonstrations of many styles and masters, followed by everyone eating and drinking leisurely over a sumptuous dinner banquet, topped off by singing and dancing together in jubilation.

Cheng Sifu never cared about the who, what, when, or where of your martial art. He accepted all martial art styles with a warm welcome. He was a kungfu cultural icon and recognized widely

Grandmaster Cheng Wan (glasses) was one of kind. His secret of aging was to remain young at heart.

as the Chu Gar Mantis headmaster in Hong Kong. Even so today, some years after his passing in 2009, when one mentions Chu Gar, Cheng Wan Sifu's name inevitably comes up.

At his request, I made the tea ceremony and became his pupil by ceremony. We were closely associated for the last decade of his life and I was appointed, in a long line, as standing Chairman of the Hong Kong Chu Gar Mantis Association.

He not only left me with the Shrine, but also, charged me with carrying Chu Gar boxing forward another generation. Moreover, he entrusted me with more than one hundred hours of Chu Gar video programs dating back to the 1950s.

MantisFlix™ Video eBooks and this book are both dedicated to his kind-hearted, open and friendly manner. They are the fulfillment of his wish for Chu Gar Mantis boxing to carry forward.

Cheng Sifu was old fashioned and yet hi-tech. He was Hakka with International friends. Fewer and fewer are the masters of the old tradition today, even here, in China. –RDH

Southern Mantis Ancestral Shrine

Chu Gar Praying Mantis Kungfu Creed

Hoc Yurn; Hoc Yi; Hoc Kungfu

學仁　學義　學功夫

Jurn Jow; Jurn Si; Jurn Gow Do

尊親　尊師　尊教訓

Respect the Ancestors for their transmission of the art.

Respect the Sifu for his teaching.

Respect the Older Brothers for their dedication and loyalty.

Respect the Younger Brothers for determination in training.

Contents

Dedication vii
Creed ix
Preface xii

Personal Records
Sifu (Gene) Chen Ching Hong 15
    Chu Gar planted in America 15
    1976 Hong Kong Chu Gar Association 16
    Martial Arts of China Chu Gar article 20; Errata 28
Sifu Yip Sui 30
    Lee Kwun Sifu 31
Chu Gar Past Masters in Charge 35

Chu Gar Mantis in Hong Kong and China
Cheng Wan Sifu - A Kungfu Cultural Icon in Hong Kong 36
    Lao Sui's re-interment 39
    Chu Gar History 41
    Chu Gar Transmission 43
    Chu Gar Hands 46 - 53
Cheng Kwun Chiu Sifu
    Abridged Interview 54 - 57

East River Chu Gar Mantis
    Variations in the Transmission 59
    Commonalities in the History 60
    Six Chu Gar Areas in China 60
    Three Kinds of Chu Gar Boxing 61
    East River Faction Conclusions 61

The Chu Gar Boxing Skills
    Principles 66
    Fundamentals 67
    Song of the Body Posture 68
    Footwork Patterns 69
    Chop Step 70
    Circle Step 71
    Straight Step 72
    Three Steps Forward 72
    Turnaround Steps 73

Contents

Single Bridge Grinding Hands 74
Dui Jong - Double Bridge Strengthening 75
Dui Jong - Mang Dan Sao 78

Dong Yat Long Sifu - Boxing Applications 80
Mang Dan Sao 81
Ying Sao Shadow Hand 82
Gow Choy Hammer Fist 83
Locking Hands 83
Bridge, Tan Sao and Ginger Fist 84
Double Bridge Gwak Sao 84
Bao Zhang Palm Sticking Hand 85
Bao Zhang Palm Intercepting Hand 85
List of principles, defensive hands, and offensive hands 86

Hakka Chu Gar Forms
List of Chu Gar Forms 87
Pictorial - Som Bo Gin, Three Step Arrow 89 - 118
Pictorial - Som Gin Yu Kiu, Three Arrow Shaking Bridge 89-129

Hong Kong Chu Gar Mantis Martial Art Assn. Photos 130 - 131

Miscellanies 132
Note on Hand names and Translations
About Southern Mantis on the Internet
About the Photographs in this book
A Final Note 133

Resources 134
China Southern Praying Mantis Kungfu Survey™ 134 - 137;
MantisFlix™ Movies and Events 138; Eighteen Buddha Hands;
Kwongsai Jook Lum Temple Hardcover Book 139; Our family
of websites 140 - 141; Instructional Playing Cards 142 - 143;
Instructional DVDs 144; Join a School or start a Study Group 145

Author's Bio 146

Study Hakka Mantis and Unicorn Culture in China 147
Cheng Wan Sifu's last public demonstration 148 - 149

Preface

In the 1970s and early 80s, Kwongsai Mantis Sifu Louie Jack Man and Master Gin Foon Mark both spoke freely about Southern Praying Mantis being a "three branch" Art from one root. Chu Gar Praying Mantis is one of those branches.

A student of Sammy Wong, in the USA, circa 1980, occasionally trained what he called, "Chu Gar," in Mark Foon Sifu's school, downtown Minneapolis. He was much harder in his single and two man training than Mark Sifu's students, but I didn't mind training with him. Not many others would, and they often said he was stiff, like Karate.

That "Chu Gar" group still exists today, in the USA, and their training is good, but as you will see in this book, it isn't traditional Chu Gar as taught in Hong Kong or China. In fact, the origin of that teaching is said to be from Sammy Wong's master named, Wong Yuk Kong. Oddly, in Hong Kong and China, Wong Yuk Kong was known as the head of Kwongsai Mantis, not Chu Gar! And, the Sombogin–three steps form that Sammy Wong taught does contain technique that can be seen in Huizhou Kwongsai Mantis!

I say this to show how easy a "one root–three branch" Art can become intermixed and misunderstood, even to the point of "four branches" when we include "Chow Gar" today.

Although there is a standard transmission that is recognized as the original Chu Gar transmission in Hong Kong and China, intermixing has been common in China, too, and variations of the Chu Gar standard abound, especially, in Singapore and Malaysia. Those who do not follow the standard may be scoffed at, in China.

With three branches (Kwongsai, Chu, Iron Ox) of Southern Mantis coming from one root, naturally there is crossover, with all three sharing similar principles, fundamentals and training.

The similarities are seen in everything from the horse posture, hand skills and form training, to the numerology and symbolism. Some turn the front foot inward, pigeon toe, others straight. Some call the hands by different names and sequence the forms differently, but,

Preface

when you can see and grasp the big picture of "one Art–three styles; one root–three branches," there are more similarities than differences. After all, people only have two hands and two feet and "Mor Sao" is still a feeling hand by any other name. (Refer to page 61, three variations of Chu Gar Mantis in China.) All the tree branches are nourished from one root.

Having stated that, we should consider that one should drink as close to the well as possible, in order to avoid polluted water. One should endeavor to receive the original transmission of the Art as close to the source as possible. It is always desirable for the Art to blossom in its pure and original form. The broader one's experience, the more one sees, the deeper the understanding that one can internalize in training. Search and prove all things.

RDH
Pingshan Town,
Guangdong, China
Summer, 2012

"Without a root,
there can be no standard.

Without a standard to follow,
the branches cannot blossom.

One must nourish the roots."

Chu Gar Mantis
Personal Records

Chen Sifu
1938 -2001

Late Sifu Chen Ching Hong

Chen Plants Chu Mantis in America, 1975

In 1975, Master Gene Chen received certification as the first teacher of Chu Gar Praying Mantis in the United States. This certificate was awarded by popular vote of the Chu Gar Tong Long Guoshu Association of Hong Kong. Association Chairpersons were Sun Yu Hing, Dong Yat Long, and Zhang Sing.

Sun Yu Hing was a right hand man of Lao Sui, one of a small band of Lao Sui's direct disciples. Lao Sui popularized Chu Gar in Hong Kong, circa 1930s. Sun was one of the prominent and distinguished Chu Gar Mantis players of the first order. Sun's student, Dong Yat

15

1976 Chu Gar Mantis Cheng Wan Martial Art Association, Hong Kong

Cheng Chiu

Chu Kwong Hua

Sun Yu Hing

Cheng Wan

Long, was Gene Chen's teacher. I met Chen Sifu while living in San Francisco. I was publishing Internationally distributed martial arts magazines and asked him to contribute articles to the magazines. He did so regularly.

He had opened a Chu Gar school there in the mid 70s with good success. That was the Bruce Lee era and San Francisco was the USA mecca for martial artists. He accepted only three Chu Gar disciples, to my knowledge, and taught us sparingly in a very traditional way.

I invited Chen Sifu to appear on the cover of Kungfu Magazine. By an unfortunate mistake, I allowed Henry Yee to be on the cover that Chen Sifu should have appeared. It was a mistake I later regretted. And I'm sure that Chen Sifu was unhappy about it.

Pin Kiu
Horizontal Bridge

He said he met his Chu Gar teacher, Dong Yat Long, when he was just a middle school kid, in 1953. Dong was a cook at middle school and the young Chen repeatedly asked him to join his Chu Gar class to no avail. It was not until Chen's mother accompanied him with gifts of wine, cigarettes, and food that Dong took on the young Chen as a student.

After emigrating to the USA with his family, in 1959, Chen Sifu continually returned to Hong Kong to study more. He stated that during a Chu Gar Mantis dinner banquet on one such return, Yip Sui had taken him to the side and taught him privately a 'secret set'. And when the bill came due, there wasn't enough money to pay, so Yip Sui gave up his watch to the inn

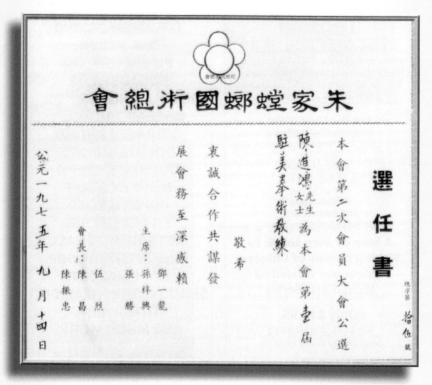

The 1975 Certificate authorizing Chen Sifu to teach Chu Gar in the USA.

keeper to settle the bill. He had high regard for the late Master Yip Sui.

Chen and his family came to the USA in 1959 by ship, and it was a long voyage. To pass time, he trained Mantis on deck. There he made friends with a Tai Chi teacher who played Yang style daily. Soon, they became friends.

The Tai Chi teacher turned out to be none other than Choy Kam Man, the chief disciple of Yip Sui in the 1950s. Choy Sifu's father, Choy Hok Pang, was born in 1885. He was a Chinese secret agent and had learned Tai Chi directly from Yang Cheng Fu.

On the boat over to America, Choy taught Gene Chen the Yang style 108 and also improved Gene's understanding of Yip Sui's Chu Gar. Gene became a student of Choy Kam Man just by coincidence of being on the same slow boat from China. I became a disciple by ceremony of Gene's Chu Gar and also a student of Choy Kam Man Sifu's Southern Mantis.

Choy Sifu never referred to Yip Sui's teaching as Chow Gar. He always said Chu Gar. I published some articles for Choy Sifu in my magazines promoting his Tai Chi legacy. He literally had taught more than 2,000 students in San Francisco Chinatown.

Choy Sifu was President of the Chinatown Photography Association and several nights a week, after hours, we would go down to the Association where he taught me his Chow / Chu Gar

Choy Sifu, chief disciple of Yip Sui in the 1950s

from his master, Yip Sui. He and Gene remained friendly and I kept in touch with Choy Sifu until his passing, in 1994.

Gene Chen Sifu was a dedicated martial artist. That's what he did. He ate, drank and slept martial arts. He had extensive notes on Chu Gar and films. When teaching, he would often go to bring out his notes. We only ever trained one on one. Although he had many Tai Chi students and disciples, there were no other Chu Gar students.

That is because, in the early eighties, Chen Sifu stopped teaching Chu Gar and began teaching Chen Style Tai Chi Chuan. He stated that Mantis was too dangerous to teach openly. And it was also very difficult to cultivate.

I once was his emissary to deliver a letter to Feng Zhi Qiang, his Chen's Tai Chi Sifu, in Beijing. I went to Feng's home in Beijing, circa Winter 1990, and the first thing Feng wanted to do was cross hands. Chen Sifu had told him I enjoyed crossing hands. Later, Feng and I, accompanied by a few others, went out for a big dinner and heavy spirits drinking. Feng was fond of spirits. We were all red-faced.

Chen Sifu and I used to go out for Dim Sum breakfast and tea every Sunday at the same location. He was well known and the cafe was

RDH–Chu Gar ceremony circa 1989

frequented by many San Francisco martial artists who always greeted each other as brother-friends.

I wrote the following article for my teacher, the late Gene Chen, in 1989, and then published it in my Martial Arts of China magazine, 1991. Unfortunately, the article contains many errors that have since come to light.

One such error in the article is the idea of a Chu Gar mantis student breaking away to create Kwongsai Mantis when he wasn't allowed to appear in a movie in which Chu Gar was defeated. In fact, just the opposite happened (as explained below). You are <u>forewarned</u> about the article. Search and Prove all things.

Hakka Praying Mantis
Chu Gar Gao: The Real Southern Mantis Boxing

Martial Arts of China Magazine, 1991
Roger D. Hagood for Sifu Chen Ching Hong (Eugene Chen)

Chu Gar Gao (Chu family creed) is a way of boxing developed with one purpose in mind: destroying the enemy. Understand that Chu Gar was created by the Ming Emperor's family (Chu Fook To) to serve the Ming Dynasty at a time when the Ching (Northern Manchurians) had invaded and taken control (1644 AD). Restore the Ming; Overthrow the Ching, was the primary purpose of the Chu Gar Style and the slogan of the day. It was the ruthlessness, bloodshed, and violence of the Manchu rulers as they hunted down and destroyed revolutionaries of the Ming dynasty (Chu family) that caused Chu Gar to develop into a direct, deadly, military fighting style–destroy the enemy before being destroyed.

Chu Fook To, of the Ming imperial court retreated to the sanctuary of the Northern Shaolin monastery and in pursuit the Ching court burned Songshan Shaolin forcing Chu and the Ming loyalists to flee southward where they settled at Fukien Shaolin with Chu Fook To becoming abbot and changing his name to "Tung Sim" (anguish) due to his deep anguish and hatred for the Ching's reign of terror and suffering. It was during this time that the Chu family boxing style was nicknamed "Southern Praying Mantis" in order to confuse the style with the Northern Shandong Mantis styles and avoid the persecution of the Ching soldiers.

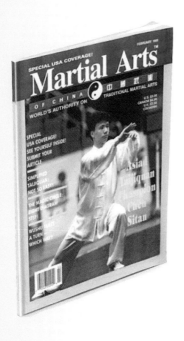

The Chu family and Ming Loyalists who fled from the north southward became known as the Hakka (Ke-ren or guest people) in South China. The style was kept a Hakka secret as it passed generation upon generation, until 1949, when Lao Sui, the Grandmaster who brought Hakka praying mantis to Hong Kong, taught the first non-Hakka generation. A non-Hakka named Yip Sui became his son-in-law.

From the time of Chu Fook To, the Chu family boxing passed to Lam Pok Koon who taught Chu Nam Chea, who then settled in Guangdong province.

At this time the "South Mantis" followers were enough to form a large army and became recognized as a "para religious sect" or Chu Gar Gao. Others such as Wong Chun So, Wong Wo Wing and Wong Wo Chek, continued to propagate Chu Gar down to Lao Choi Koon who during the Tai Ping (boxer) rebellion, in the early 1900s, taught the militiamen how to fight.

Still others such as Yuen Chun, Kwai Chi Bong, Hon Loy Chung, Lee Mok Long carried the style to the present with great distinctions. The style, as it is known today, in the USA and Hong Kong, is primarily due to the brothers Lao Sui and Lao Fu Yuen

Pin Kiu
Horizontal Bridge

who settled in Hong Kong in 1915. Lao Sui opened the style in 1949 in Hong Kong, when his five disciples each separated and created three separate streams within the style. Chu Kwong Hua was Hakka, Chu Yu Hing was Hakka, Lum Hua was Hakka, Wong Hong Kwong was Hakka and Yip Sui who married Lao Sui's daughter became the first non-Hakka to learn the system of Chu Gar Gao.

After Lao Sui's death, his son-in-law, Yip Sui created the second stream known as Chow Gar, named after Chow An Nam, who he proclaimed was the first ancestor of the style. Kwongsai Jook Lum Southern Mantis became a third door of the style, when a student of Lao Sui, in Hong Kong, wanted to make a movie, in which Southern Mantis would be defeated. When Lao Sui would not approve, the student broke away, to create the Kwongsai Jook Lum branch of the style. Thus today, we know of three Southern mantis styles with one origin: Chu Gar, the original, Chow Gar created by Yip Sui, and Kwongsai Jook Lum created by Lao Sui's student.

I (Chen Sifu) began to learn the Chu Gar style, in 1953, from Sun Yu Hing's top disciple, Dong Yat Long, who was a cook at a local school. I was only a school boy then and when I approached Master Dong, he at once refused to teach, denying any knowledge of the art.

However, through persistence and after approaching him again with my mother by my side, and making offerings of chicken, pork and wine, I was finally accepted and introduced to Sun Yu Hing. Under his tutelage for 6 or 7 years, the learning was slow but precise, and it was at this time Choy Kam Man, a student of Chu Yu Hing taught me Yang's Tai Chi.

In 1959, along with my family, I moved to the USA and it wasn't until 2 years later that I returned to Hong Kong to see Master Dong Yat Long and the Chu Gar family. During that time I trained with Yip Sui, Sun Yu Hing and Dong Yat Long and after six months training returned to the USA.

The next year, 1962, I returned to Hong Kong and saw all the Chu Gar family but Yip Sui. I spent several months there. It wasn't for three years that I would return again to see everyone (except Wong Hong Kwong who had passed away). In that year, 1965, Dong Yat Long gave a big banquet and Lum Hua, Yip Sui and Sun Yu Hing were all in attendance. During the banquet Yip Sui invited me to visit him the next day and I did so carrying gifts of herbs and teas. In exchange, Yip Sui passed some Chu Gar sets on to me as a gift. His student, Ho Ju Yuan, was still around at that time and our friendships increased.

In 1970, Master Dong Yat Long conferred on me the title of Chief Instructor with a certificate and Sun Yu Hing granted the title of Instructor with certificate in 1971. During the 1970s, I returned to Hong Kong several times to visit my old teachers, classmates and friends and during this period I began to teach Chu Gar in the USA to a few selected students. In 1975, I stopped teaching the style due to increased interest and because I felt I couldn't teach the style to just anyone because it is primarily focused on fighting.

The Chu Gar style is a complete system and is very dangerous. You learn to fight in a short time of training. It is an internal style capable of delivering internal force similar to a coiled spring that has explosive force when released.

Although recognized as an in fighting style with the ability to explode power in any direction from short distances, the system's method also extends the arms longer than most northern styles by constantly rounding the back and stretching the arms, shoulders and rib cage and also by shifting body angles for extension. Hence, the ability to use explosive force at shorter and longer than usual distances.

23

Basic training of this style consists of following the guiding principles such as sink, float, spit and swallow; (hunch back)

rounding the back like a woven rice strainer; legs must have the ability to leap like a frog and maneuver like a tiger; no T stance and no 8 stance; punch straight from the center line and standing beggar style with open hands.

The most important aspect of training is known as two man feeding. Feeding hands is the constant teaching of feeling and sensitivity, yielding and redirecting incoming power with mantis hand methods and simultaneously striking back with explosive force. Feeding hands is known as 'push hands' in Tai Chi but follows different patterns in Chu Gar with a different emphasis.

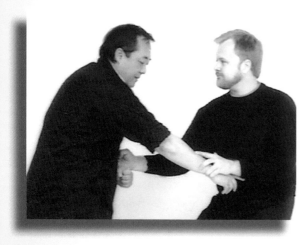

Feeding hands employs circular movement which appears soft and is generated from the dan tien, below the navel, as a pent up spring force, all the sudden released with devastating explosive power and impact as hard as iron.

When feeding hands the emphasis is to never lose contact of the

Photos: RDH and Chen Sifu feeding hands, circa 1989

opponent. As long as you can feel the enemy you can control him, and turn his power against him. This is known as making a bridge.

Feeding hands trains one to become extremely fast and alive, that is, able to react to the enemy's power. The majority of styles don't have this 'live power' and their power is dead power, that is, once an attack is launched there is no ability to change until completely executed or no ability to react to the enemy's immediate counter power. Feeding hands includes lower limbs as well.

Auxiliary training in the style contains rolling iron bars along the arm 'bridges', using the iron rings along the forearms, training finger strength by special methods of throwing and grabbing sandbags, and use of a medicine ball to strengthen the whole body.

Chu Gar is an internal style. It follows internal principles and it borrows the enemy's strength and uses it against them. The fist is also different and is known as "Feng An" or phoenix eye. This allows maneuverability in very quick action. It might be referred to as "acupuncture boxing" due to the fact that the middle index knuckle is used to strike vital acupuncture centers in rapid succession without pulling back to a chambered position. Coupled with the internal spring power the Mantis strike becomes deadly.

Compare a normal fist strike to a Mantis fist strike. A normal fist has a large surface area and when it strikes the rib cage, for example, it does great damage to the outside of the body, bruising the outer muscles and tendons. In contrast, the Mantis fist used with the internal explosive force created during feeding hands exercises, goes between the ribs in a focused way doing damage to the outside of the body but also leaving the internal organs bruised and damaged.

On Guard

Double
Beggar's
Hand
Posture

A practical example of this difference can be seen when striking a heavy cardboard box. Set the box on a table and strike it with a normal closed fist and watch the result. Then strike it with the Mantis fist or with a single finger penetration. The latter is focused and creates a single small hole. Couple this strike with the internal spring force and knowledge of acupuncture and Chu Gar becomes deadly.

Learning the Chu Gar style is like learning to drive a car. You learn how to steer, how to brake, how to turn, how to accelerate, etc. In the beginning, each is a task which needs concentration. But after a while, you perform all the operations of driving without conscious effort. So it is with learning kungfu. You learn the basic footwork of the style, the basic hand technique, the forms, the feeding hands, etc, until you perform the movements shifting weight side to side, forward and backward while employing the lightning fast hands of catching, holding, clasping, pressing, spearing, flicking, slicing, chopping, hooking, poking, and exploding fingers without conscious effort.

Chu Gar fights from an upright position, never too low to impair response and speed. Using the feeling hands of the mantis, the Chu Gar boxer closes the gap, crosses the bridge, feels his enemy's power, yields, then with the weight of the whole body and the explosive power of internal energy concentrated into one small area, destroys the enemy within one exchange that doesn't stop until blood is drawn.

Practicing Chu Gar makes one aggressive in nature. And the constant rubbing, feeling, and turning of power acquired during feeding hands gives one confidence to defeat the enemy. Because of this I do not teach the Chu Gar openly today. Even when teaching, there are many techniques which are taught only to disciples within the family.

Chu Gar is a lost art. Few Masters remain and they have no interest to publicly teach this style. It is for this reason that I have considered to preserve and teach the basics of this rare military art through books and video tape, however, I have come to no satisfactory conclusion to do so.

Single
Beggar's
Hand

As a member of the Chen's family of Chenjiagou village, I have mastered Chen style Taijiquan and today teach Chen's Taiji in the San Francisco Bay area. Having Chu Gar as a foundation was of great benefit, but in today's society we do not need to concentrate on fighting or overthrowing the officials. Chen's Taiji is also a highly effective and deadly combat art, but it is much more. It is a way of life teaching harmony, relaxation and tranquility. A way of adapting to life's complexities.

Sifu Chen Ching Hong (Gene) was born in 1938 in Shanghai, China. A member of the Chen's family village, he is a Master of the Chen's Taijiquan and President of Chen's Taiji Association in the USA Sifu Chen is also one of only a handful of Masters recognized and certified as an Instructor by Lao Sui's Chu Gar Hakka family.

February, 1991, San Francisco, California, USA
By Roger D. Hagood for Gene Chen

As seen in this (damaged) photo, Chen Sifu had many Tai Chi disciples by ceremony, but only two Chu Gar; Percy to Sifu's left and RDH behind Chen Sifu.

Although, my time with Chen Sifu was cut short, his Chu Gar teaching was a solid step for my Mantis. Sifu Eugene Chen passed away in San Francisco on June 5, 2001, at the age of 62.

Errata

The historical data in the article above was provided to Chen Sifu by his teacher, Dong Yat Long. Much of the data is not verifiable in China today. And the article contains errors. You were forewarned.

The most obvious error in the article above is about a movie that caused Kwongsai Mantis to be started by a student of Lao Sui. In fact, the truth is just the opposite. A Chu Gar student became a Kwongsai Mantis student of Wong Yuk Kong!

The movie was "Wong Fei Hong and the Jook Lum Temple." It was released in Hong Kong circa 1956. The producer was Zheng Guang Hai, who was a student of Wong Yuk Gong's Kwongsai Mantis in Pingshan Town. The tall main Mantis actor was Zheng Zhen Hua, who was a Chu Gar Mantis student of Chu Kwong Hua, successor to Lao Sui.

Chu Gar actor, Zhen Hua, after the movie was completed, became a grand student of Kwongsai Mantis under Wong Yuk Gong. Although, the movie calls and shows the banners of Kwongsai Mantis, the actors were Chu Gar at the time.

This was the very movie that started the idea of a Chu Gar mantis student breaking away to create Kwongsai Mantis when he wasn't allowed to appear in a movie. **It is fiction.** It is erroneous.

Again, this shows how easy a "three branch–one root" Art can be intermixed and misunderstood.

Remember, Chung Yel Chong was already teaching Kwongsai Mantis, circa 1917, in Hui Yang, Wong Yuk Gong in the 1930s, Lam Sang in the 1940s in the UK and USA. This movie was produced and released 1954-1956. **Search and prove all things!**

Refer to (page 134) the hardcover book "Pingshan Mantis Celebration" for historical photographs of Kwongsai and Chu Gar Mantis combined events, including Chu Kwong Hua, Yip Sui and Wong Yuk Kong, among many, socializing together.

Refer to www.MantisFlix.com to view the movie.

In 1989, Chen Sifu gave me the list below, of Hong Kong Chu Gar masters, and encouraged me to go and visit them. Many of them had already passed in 1989. On this list, of nine old style Chu Gar masters, all but one have passed today.

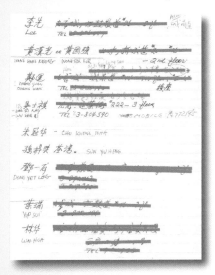

That same year, I went to Hong Kong, and called on all of them. In those early days, some simply would not see a foreigner (non-Chinese). It took persistence to open doors.

One who accepted me into his home was Sifu Yip Sui.

Grandteacher Yip Sui
1913 - 2004

Late Sifu Yip Sui

One Root Splits Into Two Trees

W hatever history has recorded as the Chu / Chow dispute, one fact is clear. Yip Sui was a disciple of Lao Sui. All other Lao Sui disciples stated, and continue to state, **Chu Gar Praying Mantis**.

None except Master Yip stated Chow.

I first visited Grandmaster Yip in his Hong Kong home, circa 1989. It was a very traditional kungfu encounter.

Our meeting was arranged by a Mr. Fok, who was heading Olympic Sports in Hong Kong. Fok was from the 9th richest family in Hong Kong and had a love for sports and martial arts. I was publishing Martial Arts of China magazine from Beijing and was introduced to Fok for cooperation. I asked him to give Yip Sui a call. He called on the spot and within a short taxi drive I was standing at Yip Sifu's door.

RDH and Yip Sui circa 1990

He and Simu, his wife, were relaxing in the early afternoon and I rang the bell. After the third ring, he opened the inner door and invited me in, although, he didn't know me at that time.

He invited me to strike him in the throat, kidneys and abdomen. He did a few dozen pushups and then ran in a small circle round and round. He explained the finer points of Sombogin form and we crossed a few easy hands to get his point across. I left with the feeling of a traditional kungfu spirit.

Later as time passed, I called on him several more times often carrying letters, tapes, or messages from Choy Kam Man in the USA, to Yip Sifu in Hong Kong. (Refer to page 19.)

Interestingly, Lee Kwun Sifu in, New York City Chinatown, is a relative of Yip Sui. Lee had a bookstore there. Yip Sifu had given me Lee's telephone number and asked me to contact him when I was back in the USA. Lee was the person with Yip in Yip's small book on "Chow Gar" published around 1960.

Several of Lam Sang's first generation disciples had also trained 'Chow' Gar in NYC as passed down from Lee Kwun to Nai Dan. Particularly, Jesse Eng Sibok and Harry Sun Sibok were friendly with that clan and shared with me their experiences. They held Yip Sui's teaching in high regard and stated that his teaching

Photos circa 1990 by RDH

could bring out the inner strength. Chow Gar was strong with a quiet but dedicated following in the NYC Chinese community, circa 1990.

As of this writing, in 2012, the Chinese community in Hong Kong and China, is becoming more vocal about the fact that Chow Gar is simply Chu Gar by another name. Yip Sui learned Chu Gar from Lao Sui and only Yip called it Chow. (Refer to page 62.)

However, no reason exists, today, not to speak of Chow Gar as a distinct and distinguished style on its own.

Through Yip Sui Sifu, Chu Gar expanded and it continues to expand.

"Yip Sui Sifu's Chow Gar" has blossomed into perhaps the most popular, and certainly the most promoted Southern Praying Mantis Kungfu today.

No picture of Southern Praying Mantis could, would, or should be, complete without the color of the late Grandmaster Yip!

Sifu Wong Yuk Kong's
1962 Kwongsai Praying Mantis
Fitness Society Celebration

TANGLANG JIAN SHEN XUE YUAN QI LIN KAI GUANG DIAN LI
1962, TSUEN WAN, HONG KONG

Centered left of the 'Unicorn' and in VIP position is Kwongsai Jook Lum Master, Wong Yuk Kong (badge on lapel). To his right is Wang Tam Gong (Chung Yel Chong's Student), Yip Sui (in Chinese dress), Chu Kwong Hua (Lao Sui's inheritor), Chu Kwong Fang (Chu Kwong Hua's Brother) were said to be in attendance. Kwongsai, Chu Gar and Iron Ox at Wong's Mantis Society.

In traditional Asian culture, the important or senior position is left of center, not right. Left is considered the weakest gate and the senior student sits left of his master's weakest side, in order to protect and defend for him.

Chu Gar Mantis
In Hong Kong and China

Chu Gar Mantis Ancestors - Past Masters in Charge

學仁學義學功夫

尊親尊師尊教訓

Lao Sui
1879 - 1942

Chu Kwong Hua
(   ) - 1993

Cheng Wan
1926 - 2009

A young
Cheng Wan Sifu
1947

Late Sifu Cheng Wan

A Hong Kong Cultural Icon of Kungfu

C hu Gar Headmaster, Cheng Wan, was on the list that Gene
Sifu gave me in 1989 (page 29). After trying unsuccess-
fully, I finally caught up with Cheng Wan at his home, in
Hong Kong, 2002. He was well acquainted with my Chu
Gar teacher, Gene Chen and my Grandteacher, Dong Yat Long, and
so he welcomed me wholeheartedly. In fact, he opened his heart
and his hand to me completely and immediately.

From 2002, until his passing in 2009, I visited him often, usually
once a month, and called him regularly. His Hakka accent was
hard to catch, but he spoke Mandarin and that was our common
language.   It took six hours round trip, travelling by car, train, and

taxi, from my home in Pingshan Town, Guangdong to his place in Hong Kong and required crossing borders four times through Customs and Immigration with visa and passport stamps.

Every year, for 35 years, Sifu had grand kungfu events celebrating the Chu Gar Mantis heritage of Lao Sui as passed to Chu Kwong Hua. They were first class with hundreds of people from the world over in attendance.

VIP attendance was by invitation (left) and I was invited to his annual Celebrations which always included dozens of demonstrations and awards from various styles including Chu Gar, Bak Mei White Eyebrow, Dragon Shadow, Choy Li Fut, Hung Gar, Wing Chun, North Shaolin, Qigong, Tai Chi, Bagua, Xing I, and many more.

Unicorns and Lions danced and dazzled the crowds followed the annual swearing in of new students and then the kungfu demonstrations. Afterwards, Cheng Sifu treated everyone to fantastic meals, great wine and Karaoke! They were kungfu celebrations of the first order!

I regret that I did not attend all the Celebrations. I am not much for large crowds. However, that did not affect my relationship with Cheng Sifu. At the 2002 Celebration, based on my experience and expertise, he appointed me as a Chairman of the Hong Kong Chu Gar Mantis Cheng Wan Martial Art Association (Certificate shown page 38).

Soon thereafter, he requested me to "offer him tea" - that is, become a disciple of his Chu Gar Mantis heritage. The Ceremony was short and informal but meaningful.

In Chu Gar tradition, it is common to record on paper that the "of-

37

香港朱家螳螂鄭運國術體育會

H.K. CHU KA TONG LONG CHENG WAN MARTIAL ART ASSOCIATION

聘任證書

螳字第壹佰〇捌號

茲敦聘

ROGER D. HAGOOD 為本會

第廿九屆名譽會長

此聘

香港 朱家螳螂鄭運國術體育會

首席會長：馬國富
當屆會長：鄭子冠
當屆會長：袁土星
當屆會長：朱國威
當屆會長：袁啓勳

主　　席：鄭運
副主席：夏國榮
副主席：袁土有
副主席：袁進發
副主席：袁偉民
副主席：黃國利
副主席：王官勳

國術主任：夏國榮
國術副主任：鄭官超

二〇〇二年六月廿九日

fering of tea" occurred and the document is signed by the Sifu and given to the disciple. The ceremony may be witnessed by two or more people. Sometimes there are no observers.

In the years following, I introduced several of my students, both Chinese and Caucasian, to also "offer tea" to Cheng Sifu. This was honorary, symbolic of dedication and loyalty. Most of my students were in transit and did not have a chance to directly train with Cheng Sifu. However, some did train directly with him.

Looking back, I think Sifu knew his time was drawing short and he was interested to vest, in me, his Chu Gar heritage. In addition to appointing me Standing Chairman, disciple by ceremony, charging me with the shrine, passing to me his video library, he also shared completely his training, which was only slightly different from that which I trained with Gene Chen.

Cheng Sifu and I trained either in his apartment or in a local park. And we often filmed sessions. In fact, Sifu went to the park the year before his passing and purposely filmed all his forms. His friendship and transmission to me was the final rooted step in my Chu Gar lineage. Now I have to find a good student to pass on this Chu Gar transmission and heritage.

Back in 2002, for Volume Five of the China Southern Praying Mantis Kungfu Survey™ (www.chinamantis.com), I interviewed Cheng Sifu and below is what he had to say.

Chu Gar–Chow Gar

I was the successor of Chu Kwong Hua, who was the senior disciple of Lao Sui.

Yip Sui's sister was the daughter-in-law of Lao Sui, and was married to Lao Sui's son, Lao Chun Hung.

Lao Sui was first buried in a place called Ho Mun Tin.

The son of Lao Sui, Lao Chun Hung, (and a student of Lum Wan who was a Quarry Tycoon) gave the money to relocate Lao Sui's bones to Fu Shan Do.

Yip Sui put "Chow" instead of "Chu" on Lao Sui's second grave without consent.   In Hakka dialect, Chu and Chow are pronounced the same but written differently.

Since then, a new gravestone has replaced the one which was written with "Chow."

Cheng Wan Personal

I began training from the age of 21 and until I was 31, I concentrated intently. From the age of 11, I watched my elder brother, a unicorn dancer, train Li Gar Kuen. When I was 16, I moved from Hong Kong to Huiyang for farming, but couldn't support myself.

Some four years later, the Germans surrendered and everyone was very poor - there wasn't even enough food to eat, we survived on bread crust - at that time even heroes were of no use! Those were difficult times indeed!

I came back to Hong Kong and took up the job that my brother was doing, ship demolitions.

We would hang off the sides of ships by rope to disassemble them. Once, my tools were stolen and there was a

A young Cheng Sifu, Circa 1947

confrontation, in which I was accosted by some Chu Gar Mantis boxers, and I wondered what kind of kungfu is this?

Chu Kwong Hua was teaching Chu Gar Mantis at the Nam Kwok Do school and a Mr. Lam introduced me to him. But, I didn't have the money to pay tuition and only those who paid more money learned more. So, I secretly practiced myself on the wooden dummy for six months.

After I trained for six months, I met those same guys again who stole my tools and I defeated them with a lop shu grabbing hand and spring power. Afterwards, instead of enemies, we all became friends through Chu Gar Mantis.

Chu Gar History

The history of Chu Gar Mantis begins with Wong Leng. He was the Fukien Shaolin 8th Sishung

Cheng Sifu 61 years later, 2008

and responsible for collecting fire wood. One day a monkey took his robe and he followed the monkey. From this he learned "three step". Wong Leng went down to Guangdong, Wu Hua district, where he met a bean curd seller named, Chu An Nam. He stayed with the Chu family for 3 years. At first, he didn't teach the Chu family any boxing. But, after another three years he taught them what he knew and then left to Shandong where he created a northern style.

But, before he left he asked a younger kungfu brother he had met in that location to teach Chu An Nam more. And so later, Chu An Nam's succession was Chu Chun Gu, Wong Fook Hong, Wong Fook Go, Lao Sui, Chu Kwei , Chu Kwong Hua, Yip Sui, Lum Hua, Zhao

Munji, Chung Hua, Lee Wei Yi, Sun Yu Hing, and Lam Wan.

Wong Fook Go also taught Yang Sao in Hui Yang, China, at the Kuan Yin Pavilion.

Chu Gar Transmission

Lao Sui had a school at Yao Ma Tei. Chu Kwong Hua taught at Sek Hong Gun Hui, a Quarry Association.

I still teach twice a week, 3 batches of students, each batch about 6 people, a two hour class. From the age of 31 until now, I have had only two students to go out on their own to teach Chu Gar Mantis.

Every year in June, since 1974, we have celebrated Chu Gar Mantis' heritage with an annual

42

celebration. Today, hundreds of folks from all over the world come to Hong Kong to be with us.

The training consists of:

Horse Stance
Tsai Kiu
Dui Jong,
Fic Shu
Dew Sao
Som Bo Gin
Som Gin Yu Sao
Say Mun Ging Ding
Tong Long Fook Fu
Say Mun Tou Da

The emphasis, he said, was "Chu Gar Tanglang You Cha Qiao Dui Qiao" or Chu Gar Mantis differs in Bridge and Counter.

In 2005, during a visit, Cheng Wan Sifu elaborated on his curriculum as outlined on the following page.

Photos Above: RDH plays Mantis, 2002 Hong Kong Celebration

Chu Gar Boxing Curriculum Abridged

Fundamentals

Body Posture and Stance

Walk the Horse; Footwork

Tsai Shu - Grinding Hands

Dui Jong - Two Man Strengthening

Single and Two Man Hand Skills

Form Training

Som Bo Gin - the Gin is written as Arrow

Som Gin Yao Shu - Swaying or Shaking Hand

Say Mun Jin Ging - Four Gate Frightening Power

Say Mun Tou Da Tou Bu Quan -
Four Gate Sneaking Hand, Sneaking Foot Boxing

Wu Tang Lang Xia San Fu -
Five Mantids Descending the Mountain Like Tigers

The following pages show several
Chu Gar Hands of the late Sifu Cheng Wan.

Cheng Sifu and Simu, his wife.

Cheng Wan Sifu
Chu Gar Mantis Hands

Swearing-in of new Members to the Association

LATE SIFU CHENG WAN CHU GAR MANTIS HANDS

Hands are a Pair of Doors

Open The Doors And Invite Them In

HAT YI SAO BEGGAR'S HANDS

46

Redirect
Force

Slice
Don't
Bang

Close
The
Doors
And
Send
Them
Out

Inner
And
Outer
Hooks

MOR SAO
FEELING HAND

LATE SIFU CHENG WAN CHU GAR MANTIS HANDS

Mid to Lower Gate

Mantis Hook with the Outer Wrist

GWAK SHU SWEEPING HANDS

Mantis
Claw
Grasping
Skills

Upper
Mid
Lower
Gates

Target:
Nerve
Plexuses,
Blood
Vessels
Muscle
And Soft
Tissue

LOP SAO
GRABBING HAND

Fingertips,
Phoenix
Eye,
Dragon
Fist

Target:
Under
The
Chin,
Throat,
Underarms
Abdomen

**JUNG SHU
UPPERCUTS**

BIL JEE EXPLODING FINGERS

Mantis Claw Grasping Skills

Target:
Eyes
Throat
Underarms

Attack
And
Defense
Simultaneous

Poke, Rake, Slice, Grab

51

LATE SIFU CHENG WAN CHU GAR MANTIS HANDS

Twisting
Forearm
Deflection

Redirect
Force

Slice
Don't
Bang

SAI SHU ROLLER ARM

Simultaneous
Offense
and
Defense

Upper
Middle
Gates

Target:
Neck,
Clavicle,
Carotid
Artery

CHOP SAO
FINGER POKES

53

Sifu Cheng Kwun Chiu

Father to Son Chu Gar Transmission

The following is an interview of Sifu Cheng Chiu. He is the son of the late Chu Gar Mantis Grandmaster Cheng Wan. I visited Brother Chiu to make inquiries into his efforts propagating Chu Gar Mantis. As I am a disciple by ceremony of his father, I address him as "Sihing" or Brother Chiu. He is featured in the Boxing Section of this book demonstrating the fundamentals and the "Som Gin Yu Kiu" form.

RDH: Let us start with the old timers who are left in Hong Kong and China. What about Lao Sui's son?

CKC: Well, the son, Lao Hong, will be in his 90s, but I don't know how to find him today. I have not heard of his passing and so he is possibly still alive.

RDH: Your father, Cheng Wan, was my third Chu Gar teacher. I called him Sigong but he asked that I should call him Sifu since I had made ceremony with him. He once asked me to drive him to Lao Sui's ancestral home since I live only 20 minutes away. He kept in touch with them and had gone there several times of which I know. Have you ever been to Lao Sui's home in Huiyang?

CKC: First, I see you are my father's disciple in his own handwriting on this paper, so we are brothers - I am your "Si-Hing". I know that the old Hakka there in Huiyang used to call our Art "Chu Gar Gao," including Lao Sui. But, I have never visited them there.

RDH: Chu Kwong Hua was recognized as the successor to Lao Sui by the Hong Kong community at the time of succession. Does Chu Kwong Hua have any relatives alive today?

CKC: He has a son, Chu Chi Keung, who is still around, I believe. He operates a medical clinic, but does not teach Chu Gar.

RDH: The late Dong Yat Long was my grandteacher. His disciple, the late Chen Ching Hong, was my first Chu Gar Sifu by ceremony. Are any of his family still alive?

CKC: Dong Yat Long had three sons and a younger brother. The son, Dong Wai Ting, used to teach Chu Gar but I have lost contact with him for a long time. Dong Fook Hong, the brother, was also a Chu Gar master. He has only one eye and if he is still alive he should be very old.

RDH: You teach Chu Gar boxing and Unicorn Dance, correct?

CKC: Yes, I teach four Chu Gar forms, Tsai Kiu, Dui Jong and such, but not much these days because the students prefer to learn the Unicorn. So, I teach Unicorn once a week and some students also train the Chu Gar.

RDH: Do you teach exactly as your father, Cheng Wan, did?

CKC: No, I teach the original four forms but, as you know, my father also taught a fifth form, "Wu Tanglang Xia Shan Fu" - "Five Mantids Descend the Mountain". It is a fighting form that covers the four corners using Lop Shu grabbing and Gow Choy hammer fist. It has been demonstrated many times even on Hong Kong television and for a time was the standard for public demonstration.

RDH: How many others of your father's students are teaching Chu Gar Mantis today?

CKC: Wu Yin Fat, a student of my father, Cheng Wan, is teaching in USA. There is another in Holland. These students are very old students. But, none other of our 'Chu Gar Pai' are teaching here in Hong Kong, now.

RDH: How long do you take to teach your students the system?

CKC: It depends on the students - some are slow and some are fast in their interest and ability. One needs at least six months to learn the four fundamental forms.

RDH: Did you only learn from your father or did you have other teachers as well?

CKC: I started at age 15 and have only ever learned from my father, Cheng Wan.

RDH: What are the important factors to build a firm rooted stance?

CKC: Walking the horse, freestyle circle stepping, Tsai Kui (four corners grinding arms) and Dui Jong (two man resistance training).

RDH: What "hands" and supplemental techniques do you teach?

CKC: There are 36 hands and each has 3 techniques or variations. 36 x 3 =108. An example is Gow Choy hammer fist - there is the top, inside, and outside hammer fist which is three variations.

RDH: One should train soft and relaxed. Chu Gar should be half soft and half hard. But, most I see today train very hard and tense only. What is your teaching about this?

CKC: One should be soft and relaxed until the moment of impact, when it becomes hard. We call it "Ging Tan Lik," or something like "frightening spring power".

RDH: Do you teach qigong?

CKC: No.

RDH: Do you teach "shen gong" or "spirit work"?

CKC: I have learned Mao Shan Shen Gong but I do not teach that.

RDH: What are the important attributes in learning unicorn dance?

CKC: The Unicorn is not difficult to learn, but very hard work. Unicorn Dance stepping is a low horse, while Chu Gar martial arts is high horse.

RDH: How long does it take to learn the basics of the unicorn dance?

CKC: About one year.

RDH: Anything else?

CKC: My father and I are both Hakka. The pronunciation of "Chu" and "Chow" in Hakka is the same. So, when Yip Sui asked Lao Sui about the name of the art, he thought Lao Sui said "Chow." But the Chinese character is different. However, Yip Sui's "Chow Gar" has produced better results at propagating the art because the other students of Lao Sui were never united in promoting Lao Sui's Chu Gar.

RDH: Yes, Yip Sui Sigong did a great work in spreading Chu–Chow Gar!

Interview End

To know more about Chu Gar on the East River, read on.

East River Chu Gar Mantis

Variations in History and Transmission

The challenge of history is to recover the past and introduce it to the present. Or, as Pearl S. Buck said, "If you want to understand today, you have to search yesterday."

There are a number of alternative histories written about the origins of Chu Gar, even by its own gatekeepers in China. I will elaborate briefly below.

In every scenario, there is a wandering monk at the turn of the 20th century who receives or transmits Chu Gar Mantis. More about that will follow.

Variations in the Transmission
Standard Version
Wong Leng, a Monk
Chu (Zhu) An Nam
Chu's son, Chu Jin
Wong Fook Go, a wandering Monk
Lao Sui

Wong Fook Go
is said to have
trained
several others,
including
Yang Sao, at the
Guan Yin
Pavilion,
at the same time that
Lao Sui was taught.

Ma Jiuhua Sifu
East River Chu Gar

Chow Gar Version
Sim Yan, a Monk
Chow An Nam
Wong Fook Go
Lao Sui

Very few things happen at the right time, and the rest do not happen at all: the conscientious historian will correct these defects.
~Herodotus,

East River Version
Mysterious Zen Monk
Chu An Nam
Chu Jin, the son of An Nam
Wong Fook Go
Lao Sui

Kwongsai Mantis Version
of Chu Gar
Two Originators - Wong Leng and Monk Lee Siem Yuen
Chu Bot Long
Chu An Nam
Lao Sui

Iron Ox Version
In China, same as Kwongsai Mantis Version

Commonalities in the History

A number of origin myths also exist. One prominent story has a rebel leader, after the failure of the Taiping Rebellion, changing his name to Chu and then organizing his Fukien Shaolin boxing into Chu Gar Gao, so as not to forget glory of the Ming Dynasty and its Emperor and founder, Chu Hong Wu.

However, all of the stories have some common denominators.

- A wandering monk at the turn of the 20th century

- The name Chu refers to the Ming Dynasty Emperor, Chu Hong Wu

- **Chu Gar originates after the Taiping Rebellion, 1850-1864, and before the founding of the Republic of China, 1911**

- Chu Gar originated in the paramilitary environment of "Fang Ching, Fuk Ming", or overthrow the Ching Dynasty and Restore the Ming Dynasty. This was the Shaolin Heaven and Earth Society, or "Triad" slogan of political resistance.

- The names of Wong Leng and Chu An Nam sound very similar to the names of the Chief and the Master of the Shaolin Triad Hong League, whose most certain aim was to overthrow the Ching and restore the Ming Dynasty.

Variations in the Chu Gar Boxing

Chu Gar became particularly widespread in the Guangdong Province areas of:

- Wuhua (五 华)

- Meixian (梅县)

- Zijin (紫金)

- Shantou (汕头)

- Xingning (兴宁) and Meizhou (梅州)

One story is that Chu Gar Gao was not known as Chu Gar Praying Mantis until Lao Sui was visited by Kwongsai Mantis Master Chung Yel Chong. After closing the door to compare technique, they discovered they were from the same root and thereafter that Chu Gar should be called Chu Gar Praying Mantis.

There are some in the five original locations who today still speak only of Chu Gar, not of Chu Gar Praying Mantis.

Three Kinds of Chu Gar

- The high horse (stance) school passed by Chu An Nam is famous in the Chaozhou and Shantou areas. It emphasizes bridge strength and explosive inch power.

- The low horse school common in the Chaozhou area. It is an imitation boxing which includes two man routines of three step.

- The Maoshan magic school of Chu boxing is the third kind.

It is sometimes confusing to have, in the same area, three schools of Chu Gar, because, regardless of their content and heritage, **they are not directly related in origin**.

However, many schools of boxing, not only Chu Gar, incorporate the Maoshan magic or "Shen Kung" spirit power boxing into their teaching. This involves charms, incantations, and methods of sympathetic magic and superstition.

East River Faction Conclusions

Ma Ming Sen (1907-1996) was a disciple of Lao Sui from the Huizhou area. His son, 71 year old, Ma Jiuhua Sifu, and a group of some 10 Teacher-Brother Chu Gar men, from Huizhou, recently made efforts to determine once and for all whether the original transmission was from the "Chu" or "Chow" surname.

Travelling to Hong Kong, they found that Lao Sui's disciple, Yip Sui, had called the style Chow Gar. It was thought to be simply a matter of the Meizhou Hakka pronunciation, in which Chu and Chow sound almost identical. And so, in late 2011, Ma Jiuhua and others travelled to Meizhou, Xingning, Wuhua and other areas to locate the very deepest root of Chu Gar.

It turned out, after exhaustive research, that Chu An Nam was the actual ancestor who transmitted Chu Gar in South China. The result was stated in Chinese:

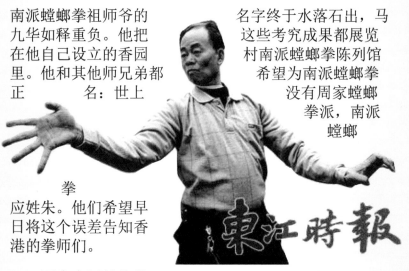

南派螳螂拳祖师爷的九华如释重负。他把在他自己设立的香园里。他和其他师兄弟都正　　　名：世上 名字终于水落石出，马这些考究成果都展览村南派螳螂拳陈列馆希望为南派螳螂拳没有周家螳螂拳派，南派螳螂

拳
应姓朱。他们希望早日将这个误差告知香港的拳师们。

因为南派螳螂拳一开始是在东江一带传承，在扬名之地香港，该拳也被叫做东江螳螂拳，马九华希望，能将此拳统称为南派东江螳螂拳，并世代在东江一带传承下去。

Ma Sifu was satisfied with their findings. There is no Chow Mantis that was transmitted in Southern China. The Mantis boxing transmitted by Lao Sui, should be surnamed Chu. Ma Sifu and the Huizhou faction wish to inform the boxers in Hong Kong of this error.

So as not to offend anyone, it is the hope of Ma Jiuhua, that this Hakka boxing may be collectively referred to as Dongjiang Mantis, and passed down for generations in the East River area.

Photo: Ma Jiuhua Sifu
©今日惠州网，天鹅城网

The Bottom Line

The present is the living sum-total of the whole past. While they still exist, we have the benefit of questioning, hand to hand and face to face, the elders regarding Southern Mantis history and original transmission. However, the elders with first hand knowledge and experience, are less and less with every day passing. Only a handful remain as of this writing.

Photo: 2008) Lao Xiangnan,
90 year old nephew of Lao Sui

The wandering Monk at the turn of the 20th century, by whatever name he is called, is likely, by preponderance of the evidence, the monk Lee Siem. Born Lee Guan Qing, he is verifiable. He was born in 1863 and fits the time line of all three branches of Southern Mantis to be the wandering monk. There are written records of his existence, including those of the Macau Temple, from 1943. Moreover, it is plausible by the boxing itself when one is able to see the bigger "one root--three branch" picture.

In the end, take your pick which history and transmission you prefer. What is important is what is available today, what of the original teaching remains, that can be transmitted to future generations.

I am not biased. I am Kwongsai Mantis and Chu Gar by ceremony and transmission. Certainly, Kwongsai Mantis and Chu Gar are branches of the same root and share a common origin and boxing techniques.

Further research is needed to dig deeper to find the oldest root and stem. Perhaps, in a future companion volume.

History is a gallery of people, places and pictures in which there are few originals and many copies. Keep the original transmission, search for the pure source. Drink close to the well.

Chu Gar Mantis:
The Boxing Skills

Principles, Fundamentals, Forms

Variations and Commonalities in the Boxing

As previously stated, the Chu Gar style is a complete system and is very dangerous. You learn to fight for self-defense in a short time of training. It is an Internal style capable of delivering internal force similar to a coiled spring that has explosive power when released.

Although recognized as an infighting system with the ability to explode power in any direction from short distances, the style's method also extends the arms longer than most northern styles by constantly rounding the back and stretching the arms, shoulders and rib cage and by shifting body angles for extension. Hence, Chu Gar has the ability to use explosive force at short and longer than usual distances.

The most important aspect of training is known as two man feeding. Feeding hands is the constant teaching of feeling and sensitivity, yielding and redirecting incoming power with mantis hand methods and simultaneously striking back with explosive force.

About the Kungfu: Principles

- Hsing-Ming Kung: The Foundation of All Kungfu

- Song of the Body Posture and Stance

- Rooting, Centering, Spiral Power

- Centerline Principle (Inner / Outer gate) (12-6; 3-9)

- Contact, Control, Strike — One Arm-Three Hands

- Intercepting and Sticky Hand

- Single - Double Bridge: Anticipating - Telegraphing

- Dead and Live Power—Lik and Ging Power

- Form and Function

- 3 Methods of Bridging: Crushing; Swallowing; Evading

- Float, Sink, Swallow, Spit

- Internal Training

- Da Mak - Dim Mak Vital Point Striking

These Southern Mantis boxing principles are outlined in detail in the "Eighteen Buddha Hands" book by Southern Mantis Press.™ Obtain the book at www.southernmantispress.com, or search for keyword "Southern Mantis Press" online at Amazon or your favorite bookseller.

One must understand and internalize these principles when beginning to train the fundamentals of Chu Gar boxing.

About the Kungfu: Fundamentals

Footwork
Opening the Horse
Shuffle Step
Turnarounds Back and Front
Chop Step
Circle Step
Advance Step
Return Steps
Chop, Circle, Advance as One
Half Steps
Side to Side Stepping
One, Two, Three Steps Forward

Additional
Kicks, Sweeps,
Takedowns, Grappling
Chin Na, Hooking
Hands, Elbow Strokes
Dui Jong Two Man Strengthening
Sticky Hand Training, Single Man Forms, Two Man Forms
Three Phases of Training

Refer to (page 139) the above book, "Eighteen Buddha Hands," for more in-depth details on Principles and Fundamentals.

Song of the Body Posture

The beginning and the end of training starts with the proper mantis body posture and stance. The song of body posture is a mnemonic device:

Legs are bent like a frog;
Hands held like a beggar (asking)
Feet look like Chinese character "ding" but not ding (page 69)
Feet look like Chinese character "ba" but not ba
Raise the perineum
Pull up the stomach

Song of the Body Posture, Con't

Open and close the rib cage
Round the shoulders
Sink the chest and raise the back
Punch from the heart
Standing beggar style with open hands
Hand to hand; Heart to heart
You don't come
I won't start
You start first
I hit first

Above
The chambered hands in front of the heart form a kind of exoskeleton with the two limbs protecting the centerline and internal organs within the torso.

Left
Place the hands akimbo when walking the horse. This keeps the hands under conscious control for the beginner and also presses downward to sink the center of gravity below the navel.

In standing, the weight is 70/30 front to rear. "Heel-to-toe" is the secret of developing the center of gravity and deep rooted posture. Posture, stance, and stepping are the foundation and source of power. Horse is father—Mor Sao grinding hand, is mother of mantis.

Stance looks like the Chinese character **"ding"** 丁
But it is not "ding"

Stance looks like the Chinese character **"ba" or eight** 八
But it is not "ba"

This means the stance is not a "T stance" as in Karate or Tae Kwon Do. And not a double weighted riding horse as in southern styles. The Mantis horse stance is something of both, but neither one.

Footwork Patterns

Boxing principles must be ingrained through fundamental training which includes footwork, two man strengthening and conditioning, hand defense and strikes, elbow strokes, kicks, sweeps, takedowns, qinna, grappling, single man forms, chi sao, two man forms, apparatus training, breathing exercises, and anatomy—vital point skills.

Traditionally, one may also become acquainted with herbal cures, bone-setting and medicinal practice and even spiritual practices of an esoteric nature.

When one has understood correct posture and internal work (horse stance), he may begin to train, "walking the horse", in various footwork patterns which may include, but are not limited to, the following. Note that still photography is not capable of capturing the motion of stepping, therefore, this section does not illustrate all stepping patterns.

Nor, is detailed instruction of the fundamental skills given in this book. Photographs and words cannot fully illustrate or teach you the dynamic "live power" of Southern Praying Mantis boxing. Seek detailed video instruction or the hand to hand, heart to heart teaching of a qualified Instructor.

Footwork - Chop Step

Technique:
1) Hands akimbo in a right horse stance. In one motion: 2) Raise the right knee up to solar plexus. 3) Back down ankle to ankle 4) Then step forward six inches while slicing out, skimming the ground toe to heel, bring up the back foot heel-to-toe on line, returning to the right horse. 5) Center, sink, & root.

Changes: Train left, right, then alternating left and right steps in one place; then train 1, 3 and 9 steps forward with turnarounds and return steps.

Attributes: One hard step makes the sound of "bing-bong."

Defense: Area from the knee to ankle (shin) defends across the centerline from solar plexus to feet. Foot instep may hook opponent's ankle.

Offense: Knee strikes (nail knees), the step down may scrape the opponent's shin and may stomp or crush the opponent's feet.

(Refer to the list of stepping patterns page 67)

Footwork - Circle Step

Technique:
1) Hands akimbo or chambered in a left horse stance. In one smooth motion: 2) Draw the right foot in a semi-circle, coming ankle to ankle, skim the ground with the toes and move forward six inches, bring up the back foot heel-to-toe on line, forming the right horse. 3) Center, sink, and root before stepping again.

Changes: Train left, right, then alternating left and right steps in one place. Then train 1, 3 and 9 steps forward with turnarounds or return steps.

Attributes: One hard step makes the sound of "bing-bong."

Defense: Area from the knee to ankle (shin) defends across the centerline from solar plexus to feet. Foot instep may hook opponent's ankle.

Offense: Hips, knees, and ankles jam against the opponent's same.

Footwork - Advance or Straight Step

Technique:
1) Hands akimbo or chambered in a right horse stance. 2) Release the coiled spring power in your stance and let it propel you forward, quickly advancing six inches toward the opponent, bring up the back foot heel-to-toe on line, returning to the right horse. 3) Center, sink, and root before stepping again.

Changes: Train left, right, then alternating left and right steps in one place then train 1, 3 and 9 steps forward with turnarounds or return steps.

Attributes: Shortest distance between two points is a straight advance step. One step makes the audible sound of "bing-bong."

Defense: Quick footwork for mobility. Advance "return step" for evasive footwork.

Offense: Chasing step to press the opponent. Stepping on the opponent's feet to render him immobile.

One Step, Two Steps, Three Steps Forward

After the fundamental Chop, Circle, and Advance steps have been trained singularly with a basic degree of skill, they may be trained in tandem with a partner to develop function and distancing. Each and all three steps may be trained by stepping 1, 2, 3, or 9 steps forward and backward. Step in unison with your partner, employing both defense and offense.

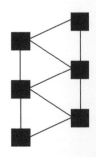

Footwork - Turnaround Steps

Turnarounds — Cross Step

Technique: Hands akimbo in a left horse stance. Step across with the front foot as shown by the arrow above. Pay attention to the position of the feet in the half turned posture. Turn around in the opposite direction. The left horse turns into a right horse behind when the turn is complete, and vice versa.

Changes: Train both left and right turns.

Defense: Evasive step and quickest turn around.

Offense: Step across is a ankle sweep or cross kick at knee level.

There are several methods of turnarounds. The above is basic and used widely in many of the single man shadowboxing forms.

Read on now, to continue the next method of training.

In-Depth Instruction

Refer to www.chinamantis.com Instructional DVD, Volume 9, for detailed instruction teaching the various footwork patterns. Also, refer to the book, "Eighteen Buddha Hands," for more in-depth details on the Principles and Fundamentals of Southern Mantis.

Single Bridge Grinding Hands

After stance training and walking the mantis horse, one should train "grinding hands." This exercise teaches bridging, feeling the opponent's power, turning power, sticking, and the development of "live power" or strength. The basic training may be called "four corner" grinding hand. One uses the strength of the whole body, isolated and issued from the elbow, pulling and pushing from shoulder to shoulder.

Start with crossed hands

1) Push and resist to the shoulder

2) Pull and resist across

3) Push and resist to the shoulder

4) Pull and resist across   1) Repeat 1 - 4 continuously

One may begin using 10% strength and with each round of 4 corners, increase by 10% until both partners are using 100% of their strength. Then reverse by decreasing strength by 10% each round from full strength back to 10%. Train both the left and right arms. This single bridge exercise is also critical to developing the stance and root. Pay close attention to the details of body posture and standing heel to toe.

Tips
- Right leg forward using right hand extended
- Left leg - left hand
- Stretch up and out - be as big as you can be
- Elbows toward ground, Grip the ground with the toes
- Clinch the molar teeth slightly, tongue up, eyes bright
- Whole body as one unit, but elbow joint turns freely
- Relax, do not be stiff

Caution–excess training of this method may injure the shoulder joints. One should next train "dui jong."

Dui Jong - Double Bridge Strengthening

After stance training, walking the horse, and single bridge grinding hands, one may progress to double bridge strengthening–dui jong. This method not only strengthens the trainees externally, it also teaches several hand skills while developing a rooted firm stance.

Dui Jong - Double Bridge Strengthening

This method may be trained both static, without stepping, and with stepping. It may also be trained single bridge using only one arm, however, it is primarily a double bridge exercise.

This is also two man training. There is an "A" side and "B" side. Each side has one step and three hand techniques as outlined below.

A - Step forward, Double phoenix eye punch, Gop Sao, Nap Sao

B - Step back, Double Jik Shu, Outside hook hand, Double Bil Jee Down

Performing "A-B" simultaneously, as outlined above, is considered **one step**. Train 3, 9, 18 or 36 steps and then reverse to train the opposite side. Going back the same number of steps, A now trains B side. B side trains A. Just switch sides. The person who stepped forward first now plays the person who steps back.

One routine is both trainees playing both sides A and B, both learning to step forward, both learning to step back for a set number of steps.

Training Tips
- Step forward on right only for one routine
- Next step forward on left only for one routine
- Alternate stepping right and left for one routine
- Stretch up and out - be as big as you can be
- Elbows toward ground, Grip the ground with the toes
- Clinch the molar teeth slightly, tongue up, eyes bright
- Whole body as one unit, but joints turns freely
- Relax, do not be stiff

Refer to the hardcover book, "Eighteen Buddha Hands" for more in-depth teaching about the individual hand skills used in this double bridge strengthening exercise.

"A" Advance steps forward, "B" steps back. Remember short steps, keeping the stance heel to toe

Train 9 steps forward and switch sides, A becoming B, vice-versa

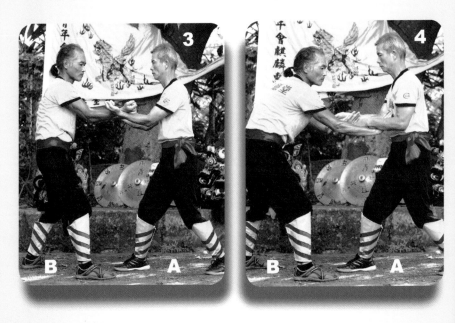

When this method is skillful, one may train the following, Man Dan Sao.

Dui Jong - Mang Dan Sao

This method, too, may be trained both static, without stepping, and with stepping. It teaches both single and double bridge exercise.

It is two man training and there is an "A" side and "B" side. Hand skills taught in this method are Phoenix eye punch, Jik shu, Pak shu, Choc shu, Bao Zhang palm, Pai shu and Mang Dan sao.

A - Step forward, right Phoenix eye punch high, Middle Phoenix Eye Punch, Tan (Choc) Sao, Palm Strike, Pai Sao

B - Step back, left Jik Shu high, Pak - Lop Shu, Palm Strike, Mang Dan Sao

Performing "A-B" simultaneously, as outlined above, is considered **one step**. Train 3, 9, 18 or 36 steps and then reverse to train the opposite side. Going back the same number of steps, A now trains B side. B side trains A. Just switch sides. The person who stepped forward first now plays the person who steps back.

One routine is both trainees playing both sides A and B, both learning to step forward, both learning to step back for a set number of steps.

Tips
- Step forward on right only for one routine
- Next step forward on left only for one routine
- Alternate stepping right and left for one routine
- Stretch up and out - be as big as you can be
- Elbows toward ground is the rule, Grip the ground with the toes
- Clinch the molar teeth slightly, tongue up, eyes bright
- Whole body as one unit, but joints turns freely
- Relax, do not be stiff

(Refer to the hardcover book, "Eighteen Buddha Hands")

Follow the A-B directions on the left (page 78)

Train right, left, alternating, so that each person may train Mang Dan Sao

This is a training reference only. It will be difficult to learn and train the methods herein without step by step video instruction or a skillful Instructor's guidance.

Join one of our Schools or Study Groups, follow step by step DVD instruction, or join me for training in China! Browse the Resource section of this book!

Late Sifu Dong Yat Long

Hand Skills - Defensive and Offensive

In Hong Kong, Dong Yat Long, his brother, and his son were well known Chu Gar Mantis exponents. Dong Sifu was a strong force in promoting Chu Gar during the 1970s. He published several articles in the Hong Kong martial arts magazines and participated in the Hong Kong Kungfu community at large as a Chu Gar Mantis representative.

Dong was a disciple of Sun Yu Hing (page 16) and the teacher of Gene Chen (page 15). Dong Yat Long was my Grandteacher of Chu Gar Mantis.

The following pictorial shows his Chu Gar hand skills. The photos are from some forty years ago and show their age.

Mang Dan Sao

On Guard
Hat Yi Sao
Beggars Hand

Opponent strikes
with right,

Mang Dan Sao -- Pull to
the side and strike simultaneously.

Follow through rapidly
with simultaneous
Pai shu to the carotid
artery and Dragon fist to
the eleventh rib.

Dong Sifu and his son,
on the following pages,
demonstrate basic appli-
cations of some Chu Gar
hands.

Ying Sao

Ying Sao is sometimes referred to as "looking in the mirror" or "shadow hand." It is striking with the back of the hand.

Top - On Guard
Ying Sao
Beggars Hand

R) Opponent strikes with right to mid section,

Simultaneously Mor Sao and strike Ying Sao

Follow through rapidly with simultaneous Mantis claws

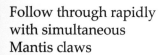

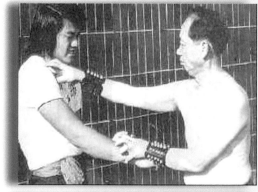

Open back to defensive Beggar's Hand posture

Gow Choy
Hammer Fist

Opponent strikes right straight to mid level

Defend with Mor Sao

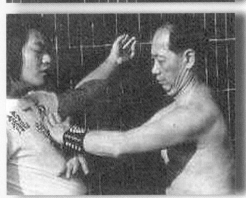

And strike over with Hammer Fist to the opponents vital points

Follow through rapidly with double palm strikes to the heart

Hammer Fist may be employed in four corners and six directions.

It is a key tool in the Southern Mantis arsenal.

Locking Hands

Left) Dong Sifu demonstrates the "Nap Sao" posture. Wrist hooks and forearms are used to lock the opponent's bridge.

Bridge, Tan Sao and Ginger Fist Strike

Close the distance and make an arm bridge,

Rapidly, Tan (Choc) Sao and strike with a slicing Ginger Fist to the mandible bone

Double Bridge Gwak Sao

Mid to lower strikes may be defending with "Sweeping Hand"

Attacks with knuckles and fingertips to the bottom of the eleventh ribs are common

Bao Zhang
Palm Strike
Sticking Hand

From a crossed hands position, one "listens" to the opponent -

Upon his first twitch of intention to attack, redirect his motion and apply Lop shu grabbing hand with simultaneous Palm Strike

Bao Zhang
Palm Strike
Intercepting Hand

From a separated distance, one must intercept the opponent's attack

Apply Lop shu Grabbing hand and Palm Strike

One must train to "intuit" the opponent's intent with both Sticky Hand and Intercepting Hand Skills

TO SUBDUE THE ENEMY WITHOUT FIGHTING IS THE HIGHEST SKILL. –SunTzu

SOUTH MANTIS PRINCIPLES	DEFENSIVE HANDS	OFFENSIVE HANDS
Warrior Spirit	摸 Mor Sao 手	Jek Shu 来复捶
Rooting	刮 Gwak Shu 手	Bao Zhang 包装手
Centering	坦 Choc Shu 手	标 Bil Jee 指
Body Posture	绑 Sai Shu 手	弹 Ping Shu 手
Footwork	食 Sic Shu 手	撞 Jung Shu 手
Ging Power	挫 Jik Shu 手	插 Chop Shu 手
Fist Methods	拍 Pak Shu 手	Gow Choy 镐捶
Solo Training	锁 Lop Shu 手	削 Jang Shu 跸
Paired Training	押 Gop Shu 手	含 Han Shu 手
Vital Points		

When drinking water,
one should drink as close
to the source as possible, as the water
becomes murky and often polluted the
further down stream one travels.
...Hakka Boxing Maxim

Form

Training single man forms and shadowboxing is to know one's self. Sticky hand and two man training is to know others.

Hakka Chu Gar Forms

There were four original forms:
- Som Bo Gin
- Som Gin Yu Kiu
- Som Bond Ging Tan
- Fut Sao Buddha Hand

By the mid 1950s the Chu Gar expanded:
- Jik Bo
- Som Bo Gin
- Som Bo Gao Choy
- Ying Chum Sao
- Som Gin Yu Sao
- Say Mun Bao Zhang
- Som Yu Som Fung
- Gan Tan Ging
- Chut Bo Tui
- Som Gong Bo
- Sup Bot Mo Jung
- Fut Sao

The late Cheng Wan Sifu was head of Chu Gar in Hong Kong. His transmission was:
- Som Bo Gin
- Som Gin Yu Kiu
- Say Mun Ging Ging
- Say Mun Tou Da Tou Bu
- Wu Tanglang Xia Shan Fu

Cheng Sifu passed December 2009 at 86. He was one generation removed from Lao Sui.

Chu Gar factions along the East River today may be found teaching:
- Som Bo Gin 三步箭
- Som Gin Yu Kiu 三箭搖橋
- Som Gin Pi Kiu 三箭批橋
- Som Gong Po Kiu 三弓迫橋
- Yin Yang Sao 陰陽手
- Fo Sao 佛手
- Sup Bot An Gin Sao 十八暗勁手
- Som Bo Lie Kiu 三步攦橋
- Chan Si Sao 纏絲手
- Po Shan Kuen 迫山拳
- Say Mun Ging Ging 四門驚勁
- Dai Sui Lian Hun 大小連環
- Chut Bo Lian Huan Ko Da 七步連環扣打
- Lian Hun Shuang Tu Sao 連環雙吐手
- Yao Loong Sao 游龍手
- Na Loong Sao 拿龍手
- Mor Pan Sao 磨盤手
- Tanglang Tu Wu Sao 螳螂吐霧手
- Sup Bot Bo Chan Sao 十八捕蟬手

The expanded curriculum came about by the 5 disciples of Lao Sui creating new sets. However, any new training MUST conform to the root, standard, and principles of the Art, and should be identified as new, not orthodox.

Som Bo Gin 三步箭
Som Gin Yu Kiu 三箭搖橋

I offer this form pictorial as a record only. It is impossible to teach form correctly by a book, but, the pictorial will serve as a reminder of the sequence. It is always best to seek a competent teacher. Step by step DVD instruction is a second choice.

If you do not understand the principles and fully train the two man fundamental skills first, then **form training** is a house without a foundation; a house built upon sand.

Your Mantis house is empty without becoming skillful at the fundamental two man footwork, two man hand skills, sticky hand and two man forms. Once these are correct, your single man form will be correct. Shadowboxing alone will lead to failure in self-defense.

Having said that, the beginning of training is by self study alone. You must ingrain the Mantis body posture and internal work and that can only be accomplished by oneself. Form is an essential self-study tool.

Important elements to remember:
- 18 points of internal training
- Natural breathing, holding the breath
- Stepping pattern
- Relaxed strength not tense and stiff
- Float, sink, swallow, spit
- Offensive-Defensive
- Three Power Gin - arrow, forward, scissors
- Warrior Intent

The following pages show step by step the primary postures, in sequence, of the first two Chu Gar forms, Som Bo Gin, and Som Gin Yu Kiu. Training from this book alone, you may first stand and hold each posture for 3-5 minutes. When you remember the sequence without fail, then you may link the postures together in "form" by movement. Seek a competent instructor or follow a DVD.

Som Gin Yu Kiu 三箭搖橋

Som Bo Gin 三步箭

L) LATE GRANDMASTER
CHENG WAN
AND HIS SON, SIFU CHENG CHIU

1

Som Bo Gin 三步箭

2

Som Gin Yu Kiu 三箭搖橋

Som Bo Gin 三步箭

3

91

Chu Gar Mantis Form Training

Som Bo Gin 三步箭

Som Gin Yu Kiu 三箭搖橋

Som Bo Gin 三步箭

5

Som Bo Gin 三步箭

Som Gin Yu Kiu 三箭搖橋

Som Bo Gin 三步箭

7

95

Chu Gar Mantis Form Training

Som Bo Gin 三步箭

Som Gin Yu Kiu 三箭搖橋

Som Bo Gin 三步箭

Som Bo Gin 三步箭

10

Som Gin Yu Kiu 三箭搖橋

Som Bo Gin 三步箭

11

Chu Gar Mantis Form Training

SOM BO GIN
REPEAT
10, 11, 12
THREE
TIMES

Som Bo Gin 三步箭

12

100

Som Gin Yu Kiu 三箭搖橋

Som Bo Gin 三步箭

13

Chu Gar Mantis Form Training

Som Bo Gin 三步箭

14

102

Som Gin Yu Kiu 三箭搖橋

Som Bo Gin 三步箭

15

Som Bo Gin 三步箭

Som Gin Yu Kiu 三箭搖橋

Som Bo Gin 三步箭

17

Som Bo Gin
18, 19, 20
Turn
Around
Go in
Opposite
Direction

Som Bo Gin 三步箭

18

106

Som Gin Yu Kiu 三箭搖橋

Som Bo Gin 三步箭

19

107

Chu Gar Mantis Form Training

Som Bo Gin 三步箭

Som Gin Yu Kiu 三箭搖橋

Som Bo Gin 三步箭

21

109

SOM BO GIN
REPEAT
20, 21, 22
THREE
TIMES

Som Bo Gin 三步箭

22

Som Gin Yu Kiu 三箭搖橋

Som Bo Gin 三步箭

23

Som Bo Gin 三步箭

SOM BO GIN
REPEAT
23, 24
THREE
TIMES

24

Som Bo Gin 三步箭

**TURN
AROUND
23, 24, 25**

25

RIGHT
SIDE
YU KIU
SHAKING
BRIDGE
IS 26–30

Som Bo Gin 三步箭

26

114

Som Gin Yu Kiu 三箭搖橋

Som Bo Gin 三步箭

27

115

Som Bo Gin 三步箭

Som Gin Yu Kiu 三箭搖橋

Som Bo Gin 三步箭

29

**REPEAT
26 – 30
AGAIN
LEFT SIDE
AND
RIGHT SIDE
BEFORE
31**

Som Bo Gin 三步箭

30

118

Som Gin Yu Kiu 三箭搖橋

32

TURN AROUND 31, 32, 33 AND STRIKE 34 BEHIND

33

34

35

36

Som Gin Yu Kiu 三箭搖橋

37

Chu Gar Mantis Form Training

38

39

Som Gin Yu Kiu 三箭搖橋

41

Hong Kong Chu Gar Praying Mantis Cheng Wan Martial Arts Association, 2008

For nearly four decades, hundreds of people internationally travelled to Hong Kong to celebrate Cheng Wan Sifu's birthday and the legacy of Chu Gar Praying Mantis Kungfu from Lao Sui to Chu Kwong Hua. Cheng Wan Sifu passed in 2009.

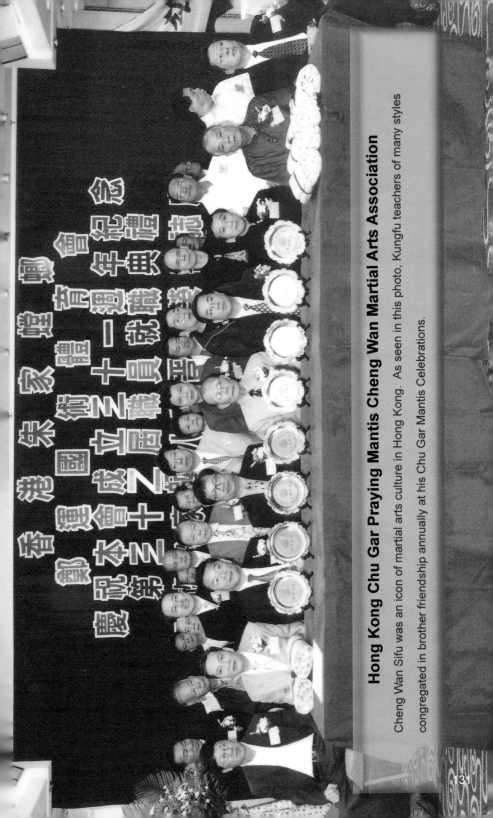

Hong Kong Chu Gar Praying Mantis Cheng Wan Martial Arts Association

Cheng Wan Sifu was an icon of martial arts culture in Hong Kong. As seen in this photo, Kungfu teachers of many styles congregated in brother friendship annually at his Chu Gar Mantis Celebrations.

Note on Hand Names and Translations
In China, everyone has their own "jia xiang hua", or home town dialect. Hakka is one such dialect and each clan or town may even have their own pronunciation of Hakka language. The names given herein, are the names that are commonly used so that everyone is on the same page and understands which skill or hand is being talked about. It is less important what you call the skills, and more important that everyone understands.

The Chinese romanization herein is the same—it is written phonetically or what is common, so that it can be easily understood. Chinese names herein are not correct pinyin, purposely.

"Shu, Sao, and Shou" all simply mean "hand" and are often used interchangeably. Remember, once the stance, root and feeling hand is skilled, the whole body is one "hand".

About Southern Mantis on the Internet
The internet and DVDs can be a great aid to learning. How much better are DVDs than secretly peeking through holes in a fence or wall to learn Mantis? In the early days, sneaking a peek through a hole was quite common.

Nothing can replace the spirit and hand of a skillful teacher. But, the new media and resources are still a valuable asset. The internet, however, is also a large source of disinformation. Repeating what someone else said erroneously often becomes accepted as SPM "truth" without verification. There is a great deal of "false" information on the internet about Southern Praying Mantis.

An example is the 'Blanco' article. Circa mid 1990s, Blanco, from Hong Kong, called my office in the USA asking how to contact Southern Mantis teachers in China. I did not provide him any information. Southern Mantis teachers usually frown on unannounced visits from strangers. Later, he "compiled" his article using sources, such as my published works, without permission.

132

Much of his article is erroneous and needs correction. I encourage you to seek the truth for yourself. Do not follow any one blindly. Search and prove all things. The further you go downstream the murkier the water. Drink close to the source.

About the Photographs in this Book

The images are from my personal library. They were not made in a studio for glamor, but made on the spot with the various Teachers herein. Appreciate the images for what they are - natural shots of Sifu, in their own elements. None of the images can be made again—those days are gone. Sadly, many of the elder teachers have passed away, as well.

Additional photos indicated ©今日惠州网，天鹅城网

A Final Note

This Volume relates to the basic history of Chu Gar Mantis. I intend to add more historical documentation and continue outlining the fundamentals and orthodox forms training in an upcoming volume.

The branches of Southern Praying Mantis are from one root. Each has its advantage and is worthy of study. Although, I am first, Kwongsai Jook Lum Temple Mantis, and second, Chu Gar Mantis, both by Ceremony and Transmission, I am not biased or preferential. They are harmonious and may be taught side by side. The only difference is the depth of the transmission one receives.

If you are interested in training Southern Mantis by DVD or coming to Hong Kong or China to study Southern Mantis, then you may email me directly. I have a class in Guangdong, China and Cheng Chiu Sifu, teaches Chu Gar and Hakka Unicorn culture in Hong Kong. Welcome!

rdh@chinamantis.com
Roger D. Hagood
Standing Chairman

Hong Kong Chu Gar Tonglong Martial Art Association Headquarters

Vol 1: Pingshan Mantis Celebration Hardcover or eBook

Pingshan Mantis Celebration
A rare book of China's Kwongsai Jook Lum Temple Praying Mantis Kungfu and Unicorn Culture.

Included are: Origins, history and practices of China's Kwongsai Mantis, rare and exclusive historical photographs never published before, the hometown of Kwongsai Mantis-Pingshan Town, how Wong Yuk Kong came to learn Hakka Mantis, why Wong Sifu went "mad" after a spell was cast, why Hakka Mantis is divided into "three orders" and what they are, three Wong Brothers who inherited Kwongsai Mantis, what Kwongsai Mantis boxing was taught early on and now, what happened when Kwongsai Mantis and Chu Gar first met, Hakka Mantis descending the mountain on horseback in 1917, English and Chinese translation of how Master Chung blossomed Hakka Mantis in South China, Hakka Culture along the East River, extensive interviews with inheritor Wong Yu Hua about sensitive topics, rules and regulations of Wong Yuk Kong's Mantis School, a Hakka Feast in

Pingshan Town, valuable Hakka Mantis resources online and off, Hakka Mantis boxing maxims and proverbs, dozens of Kwongsai Mantis boxing postures, staff, and sword pictures, rare never before published Jook Lum Mantis reliquary photographs, the Bamboo Forest Temple true heritage Dit Da liniment prescription and more.

Available at Amazon, Barnes and Noble, and other fine booksellers!
Search Keywords - Southern Mantis Press

Volume 2: China Mantis Reunion

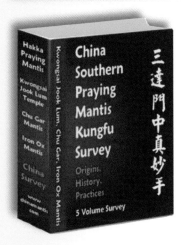

Hardcover Book
or
eBook Available Now!

www.chinamantis.com

In Volume Two:

At the request of Sifu Wong Yu Hua , a number of junior, senior and elder Southern Mantis masters, dating back to circa 1920s, gathered in Huizhou, Guangdong. It's about an hour's drive from Pingshan Town and most of the mantis brothers there had not seen each other for many years.

The gathering included those who in the 1930s and 40s, were among the in-crowd of Chu Gar and Iron Ox, as well as,

Kwongsai Mantis. Some had studied all three branches of Som Dot's teaching. Learn directly from them and see their demonstrations of boxing and staff play in Volume Two of the China Southern Praying Mantis Survey.

Get your copy today!

Volume 3: Iron Ox / Kwongsai Mantis Interviews

Hardcover Book
or
eBook Available Now!

www.chinamantis.com

In Volume Three:

Learn from Kwongsai Elder Master, Yao Kam Fat, who visited Lao Sui with Wong Yuk Kong. Watch his demonstrations of Third Door, Push Hands, and Plum Flower Pole Form. Hear stories which shed a great deal of light on Chung Yel Chong and Lao Sui's relationship, and other mantis ancestors.

Also, Iron Uncle Chung sheds light on mantis in the very earliest days, circa 1920s.

Yang Gun Ming's family interview shows the degree that mantis once permeated south China villages.

And you will discover the origin of China's Iron Ox Praying Mantis and visit with an inheritor, Sifu Xu Men Fei, as he takes you on a tour of Pingdi, an Iron Ox Village and its ancient Clan Temple. Watch demonstrations of the Iron Ox forms Second Door, Third Door, and Big Red Pole forms! Get your copy today.

Volume 4: On Som Dot's Trail / Chung Yel Chong

Hardcover Book
or
eBook Available Now!

www.chinamantis.com

In Volume Four:

INTERVIEWS
Visit Chung Yel Chong's (Zhang Yaozong), third ancestor's, family and clinic and watch his grandson perform treatments; an in-depth interview of Chung Yel Chong's family. Rare photographs.

An interview with Sifu Lee Kwok Liang in Hong Kong, who was a student of Kwongsai Mantis Masters Chang Gun Hoi and Wong Yuk Kong. Lee Sifu still teaches in Hong Kong today and his son, Patrick is a mantis Sifu, as well.

ON SOM DOT'S TRAIL
Visit Shanxi in the North and Jiangxi (Kwongsai) in the South of China where Som Dot and Lee Siem Yuen treaded. See what the old Bamboo Forest Temple located in Shanxi looks like today! And visit the bamboo forests of Mt. Dragon Tiger and the mansions of the first Taoist Pope where the "108" Demons were confined into a well.

Hear what the elders at the Macau Bamboo Forest Temple had to say about Lee Siem Yuen! And more. Get your copy today!

MantisFlix™ Video eBooks

60 Years of Southern Mantis Movies and Events!

Wong Fei Hong and the Jook Lum Temple

Volume 1001 - Hong Kong 1954

B/W Classic Movie Exclusive! 100,000 plus clip previews on YouTube. Get your full copy now!

Kwongsai Mantis Celebration

Volume 1002 - Pingshan Town, Guangdong, China

Late Sifu Wong Yuk Kong Kwongsai Jook Lum Clan 35th Anniversary Celebration, circa 2003.

Hakka Boxing Collection One
Volume 1003 - A rare collection of Hakka Boxing.

Hakka Boxing Collection Two
Volume 1004 - A second rare collection of Hakka Boxing.

Chu Gar Cheng Wan Celebration
Volume 1005 - Join the 1989 Cheng Wan Chu Gar Mantis Celebration in Hong Kong! Cheng Wan Sifu was the inheritor of Chu Gar descended from Lao Sui.

View and Enjoy Video Previews Online:
www.MantisFlix.com

Hardcover Collector's Edition Book

Eighteen Buddha Hands
Kwongsai Jook Lum Temple Mantis

A rare instructional treatise of Chinese boxing from the Kwongsai Dragon-Tiger Mountain, Bamboo Forest Temple, Praying Mantis Clan, as transmitted by the late Grandmaster Lam Sang.

Details include stories of Lam Sang's supernatural ability such as Poison Snake Staff, Sun Gazing, and Light Body Skills. Boxing principles elaborated are Body posture, Rooting, Sinking, Center-line, Spiral power, Contact-control-strike, Intercepting and sticky hand, Bridging, Anticipating-telegraphing, Dead and live power, Form and function, 4 word secret, Dim Mak vital points and more.

Boxing Fundamentals included are Footwork: Chop, Circle, Advance, Shuffle step, Turnarounds, Side to side; Kicks, Sweeps, Takedowns, Grappling, Chin Na Seizing, Hook hands, Elbow strokes, Dui Jong, Sticky hands, Forms, and Phases of training. Eighteen Buddha Hand techniques, 9 defensive, 9 offensive, are illustrated in color with instruction in attributes, function and vital point targeting. Boxing maxims of strategy and tactics are included.

Available at Amazon, Barnes and Noble, and other fine booksellers!
Search Keywords - Southern Mantis Press

Online

Our Family of Hakka Mantis Websites
Visit and Enjoy! Informational, Educational, Instructive

www.SouthernMantisPress.com

A ten year ongoing research in China
of the origins, history and practices of Southern Mantis!
Dedicated to the late Wong Yuk Kong Sifu in China!

chinamantis.com

The Bamboo Temple Association is
a mutual aid fraternity.Join us and
become a member, School, Branch or
Study Group today!Dedicated to the
late Lam Sang Sifu's teaching in the
USA.

bambootemple.com
bambootemple-chicago.com
btcba.com

These sites reveal many China
Kwongsai Mantis Sifu who have
heretofore remained silent about the teaching of Kwongsai
Dragon Tiger Mountain Bamboo Forest Temple Mantis and
outlay the lineage of Hakka Mantis as stated in China.

kwongsaimantis.com
somdotmantis.com

This site details the complete history of Chu Gar Gao Hakka
Praying Mantis as descended from the late Lao Sui in Hong Kong
and Hui Yang (Wai Yearn), China.

Resources

(con't) Dedicated to the late Cheng Wan Sifu who passed in 2009.
chugarmantis.com

This site is dedicated to the late Xu Fat Chun Sifu and speaks of
the history of Iron Ox Hakka Praying Mantis in Pingdi Town,
Guangdong, China.
ironoxmantis.com

Historical Hakka Mantis Flix! Some 60+ years of Hakka Southern
Praying Mantis Kungfu movies and events in video eBooks!
mantisflix.com

Our dedicated South Mantis Tube. We have several hundreds of
hours of videos in our Hakka Mantis archives dating back to 1950
in China that we hope to share with you!Feel free to share.Upload
your Southern Mantis or Hakka video now!
southmantis.com

Genuine Internal Work - the original 11 month correspondence
course of Tien Tao Qigong.
tientaoqigong.com

Ancient Methods to achieve vitality and a healthier well-being! The
Oriental Secrets Series of Qigong.
oss.tientaoqigong.com

And visit our daily YouTube feed of only
Southern Praying Mantis videos!
chinamantis.com/youtube

And our YouTube channel:
youtube.com/chinamantissurvey

New Media from Southern Mantis Press.com

Southern Mantis Instructional Playing Cards

Kwongsai Mantis
18 Buddha Hands

Card Backs: Various Sifu of Lam Sang's generations in multiple postures

Card Fronts: Two man application photos, Text instruction, Instructive maxims

Includes the 18 Buddha Hands and more of Kwongsai Hakka Mantis

Key Benefits
of our Card Decks

- 54 Cards with Hakka Mantis

- Customized Front and Back

- Full Vibrant Color!

- Instructional

- Educational

- Informative

- Rare and Exclusive Content and Photographs

- Entertaining - Play Hakka Mantis Cards with your friends

For ♣ A

For ♦ A

For ♠ 2

For ♥ 2

For ♣ 2

For ♦ 2

For ♠ 3

For ♥ 3

18 Buddha Hands—Instructional Card Deck

Card Deck Use Includes

- Useful gifts for martial artists
- Instructional and Informative
- Invaluable Heirloom of Hakka Mantis Masters

Card Decks Include

- 54 card deck in standard size
- Made from 100% casino quality card stock
- Clear plastic case included

Wholesale Inquiries Welcome

Other Decks Include:

- Chu Gar Mantis - "Fundamentals"
- China Kwongsai Mantis - "Celebration"

Front

Front

Front

For order info email:

cards@chinamantis.com

ChinaMantis.com   Instructional DVDs

Jook Lum Temple Mantis
Step by Step Instruction
in 18 Volumes

Year One Training
Volume One: Fundamentals; The Most Important
Volume Two: Phoenix Eye Fist Attacking / Stepping
Volume Three: Centerline Defense
Volume Four: One, Three & Nine Step Attack / Defense
Volume Five: Centerline Sticky Hand Training
Volume Six: Same Hand / Opposite Hand Attacks
Volume Seven: Sai Shu, Sik Shu, Jik (Chun) Shu
Volume Eight: Gow Choy; Hammer Fist-Internal Strength
Volume Nine: Footwork in Southern Praying Mantis
Volume 10 Chi Sao Sticky Hands and Passoffs

Advanced Two Man Forms — Year Two and Three
Available by request. Prerequisite Volumes 1– 10.
Volume 11: Loose Hands One
Volume 12: Som Bo Gin
Volume 13: Second Loose Hands
Volume 14: 108 Subset
Volume 15: Um Hon One
Volume 16: Um Hon Two
Volume 17: Mui Fa Plum Flower
Volume 18: Eighteen Buddha Hands
All 8 two man forms must be trained as one continuous set on both A - B sides.

Summary Year One
http://www.chinamantis.com/first-year-training.htm

Summary Year Three:
http://www.chinamantis.com/summary-of-training.htm

Join a School or Start a Study Group

**Bamboo Temple Chinese Benevolent Association
Hong Kong Chu Gar Mantis Martial Art Association**

**Roger D. Hagood, Standing Chairman
Hong Kong, Shenzhen, China**
rdh@chinamantis.com

USA

**Crystal Lake, Illinois School
Richard Lee Gamboa
USA Chief Instructor**
Phone: (847) 458-2080
Mantis@ActionKungFu.com

**Los Angeles, CA School
John Brown**
Phone: (510) 423 1615
Tonglong108@gmail.com

**Huntsville - North AL, Branch
Slade White**
256-694-0949
slade@sladewhite.com

**Indiana, USA Branch
Dave Marshall**
812-709-0827
ictdave@aol.com

**Washington DC Study Group
Eric Lewis**
240-552-1338
rev_ericlewis@hotmail.com

**Weslaco, TX Study Group
David Garcia**
(956) 472-0254
garciads1@gmail.com

INT'L

**Taipei, Taiwan Branch
Dr. Han Chih Lu**
simonclh@gmail.com

**London, Ontario,
Canada Branch
Mike Shaw**
Phone 519-852-2174
mantismike@start.ca

**Düsseldorf,
Germany Branch
Erik Irsch**
eirsch@yahoo.de

**Lima, Peru
Study Group
Guillermo E. Talavera**
getalavera@hotmail.com

**Lugansk, Ukraine
Study Group
Andrew V. Potapov**
mantis_ukraine@ukr.net

Like minded people that have a sincere interest to study Southern Praying Mantis together and are following the Instructional DVDs may start a Study Group.
Become a group leader today!

RDH Bio

Welcome to visit the Author!

Your email correspondence is welcome and do visit and study Hakka Southern Praying Mantis with me in beautiful sunny south China!   I am an Author, Publisher and Producer of eBooks, books, journals,

videos and
7 International
martial arts
newsstand
magazines in
15 countries
with 45 years
in training
and teaching
martial arts
and some 20
years living in
China and Asia!

Currently residing in beautiful sunny south China for the last 10 years where I teach Southern Praying Mantis.   Join my class in Guangdong today!

RDH
Pingshan Town, China
Summer 2012

More Bio:
http://www.chinamantis.com/roger-d.-hagood.htm
Email:
rdh@chinamantis.com

146

147

AT LATE SIFU
CHENG WAN'S
LAST PUBLIC
DEMONSTRATION,
THE CROWD
ADORED HIM AND
HE LOVED THEM
DEARLY!

Cheng Wan Sifu (1926-2009)

CPSIA information can be obtained
at www.ICGtesting.com
Printed in the USA
LVIC06n2231300514
388020LV00001B/1

* 9 7 8 0 9 8 5 7 2 4 0 2 3 *